Grandpa Jones
5-String Banjo

by Mark Jones

EXCLUSIVE SALES AGENT: MEL BAY PUBLICATIONS, INC., PACIFIC, MO 63069

Visit us on the Web at www.melbay.com — E-mail us at email@melbay.com

GRANDPA JONES

Above is a picture of the author and copyright owner of the Old-Time Southern Style system for 5-string Banjo, with Moose Horn.

Contents

Preface

This is my 40th year on radio. I started back when the carbon microphone was all the go. During that time I have received hundreds of letters asking me if I had a "five string" banjo coarse, or whether I knew of one in existence. Of course I did not. Because to my knowledge there wasn't any. That is the main reason that I decided to devise one, and one to the best of my knowledge. I've made it the most simple, the easiest to understand and yet, I believe the best way to learn the "old time thumb string style" banjo. Some of the "old timers" call it "rapping" the banjo.

Pete Seeger has a fine book on the 5-string. I think that the five string banjo should be tuned to the "A" chord to give it the brightest tone. Starting with the "little" string or "thumb" string that would be; A,E,A,C♯ and E (5 4 3 2 and 1.)

Some people play this style with, as I've heard them say, a "low" bass; or the fourth string tuned down to "D". There are a number of other tunings. Some of the "old timers" had a tuning for almost every song. But I don't think that it is necessary to know but two or three.

In selecting a banjo, that is suitable to start on, there are two things that are important. If it is a used banjo, be sure that the neck isn't loose at the base. And be sure there is a good head on it - one that will tighten good. A tight head is the main thing on a banjo.

In compiling this book of instructions I have secured the services of one of the best musicians I know of that also understands the tenor and five string banjo, by the name of Dale Parker. Between Dale and me, I hope we have succeeded in compiling a book that will help you to master the old "thumb string style" of picking the five string banjo.

Sincerely,
Grandpa Jones

Fingerboard and Diagram Explanations
(Showing Use of Left Hand)

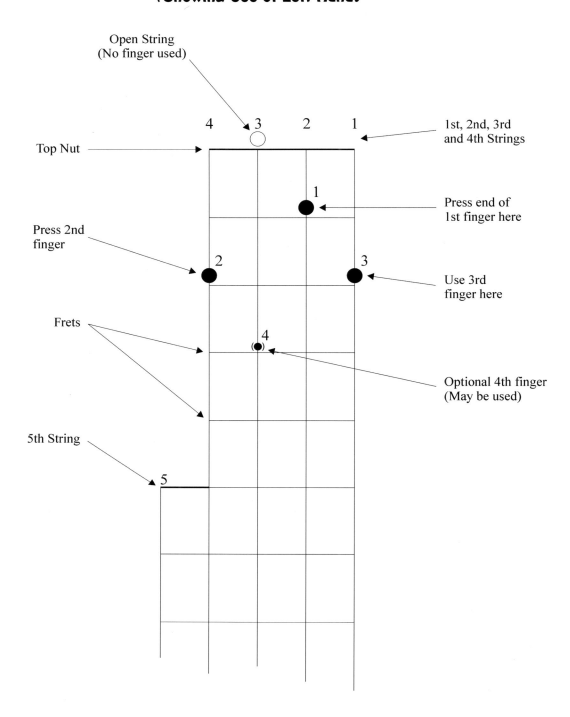

The 5th String is always played open, when rapping the banjo.

The fingers of the left hand are numbered thus: Finger next to thumb is 1st finger.

        Next finger - No. 2.   Next finger-No. 3.   Little finger - No. 4.

The "O" at top of chord-diagram indicates this string is to be played open (No fingers of left hand touching it.)

Place fingers, as indicated, just barely behind fret. Press firmly so that clear tone is heard.

Helpful Suggestions

You will find the principal chords for four different keys shown in this book. I hardly ever need to play in other keys. It is possible to play a song in any key. If you wish to sing a certain song, play the first chord shown and you should be able to get your pitch from this. If the key seems too high or too low for you to sing well try the first chord of another key and so on until you have found the key best suited for your voice.

If you wish to play the chords to any song in a different key than it is written you can refer to the transposing chart. Soon you should be able to change to another key and play the chords by ear.

It is best to learn the chords rather well before attempting to play the melody. Hum or sing the songs in this book while you practice playing the chords. Then when you begin to get a little better maybe you can play along with some other lead instrument such as a fiddle, etc.

I have found that it is better to practice a little each day than a whole lot only now and then. Don't give up too easily. Anyone has to spend plenty of time practicing and the more interest and patience you have the better your chances.

I would like to remind you to keep the calf skin or plastic head tight and also to not use the same strings on your banjo so long that they lose much of their snap and crisp tone.

Notes on Picking the 5-String Banjo

There are several styles of picking the 5-string banjo. Some use metal picks on one or more of the fingers. Some pick upward with the 1st finger, etc.

I use the old-time style of picking sometimes referred to as "rapping" the banjo.

Using a pick on the 1st finger only, I pick down. Be sure to move the entire forearm and not just the finger and wrist. For the thumb I use no pick and strike the string in the usual manner. This may seem rather complicated but practice will help you to understand and, after all, there are no set rules when it comes to picking the 5-string banjo.

Now concerning the rhythm I ordinarily use: Try practicing this with your right hand. Pick down twice on the 1st string using the 1st finger. Then with the thumb pick once quickly on the thumb string. Keep repeating and you get a rhythm something like this: Thump, Thump-a Thump, Thump-a Thump, etc.

After you have tried this awhile you can play some chords. Start with the chords in the key of "A". Be sure your banjo is tuned correctly ("A" tuning) as shown on another page. The strings are played open for the "A" chord. Pick down with the 1st finger twice on two or more of the strings. Then quickly pick the thumb string once with the thumb. Keep repeating this process. You can pick one of the other strings with your thumb every-other time if you wish. Next, place the fingers of your left hand just behind the proper frets, as shown in the diagram, to get the "D" chord. Keep picking in the same manner. Go on to the E7th chord - Then back to "A".

When you have learned to change to these three different chords without losing any time you are ready to play the chords to a song. Either sing, whistle or hum the melody while playing the chords.

A little farther on you will find instructions on keeping good time and a picking exercise.

Hand Positions

How to Tune the Banjo by Ear

Note: Keep good strings on your banjo. No string instrument sounds good with old worn out strings.

To tune 5-string banjo in "A" tuning by ear: Tune 4th string low as possible but not so low that it will rattle or won't sound clear. Then place a finger on 5th fret as shown here. Tune open 3rd string to sound same as 4th string. Then place finger on 4th fret of 3rd string tuning open 2nd string to sound the same. Next place finger on 3rd fret of 2nd string tuning open 1st string to sound the same. Then lastly place finger on 5th fret of 1st string to tune the 5th string.

You can also tune to the piano as shown below.

For playing in the key of A

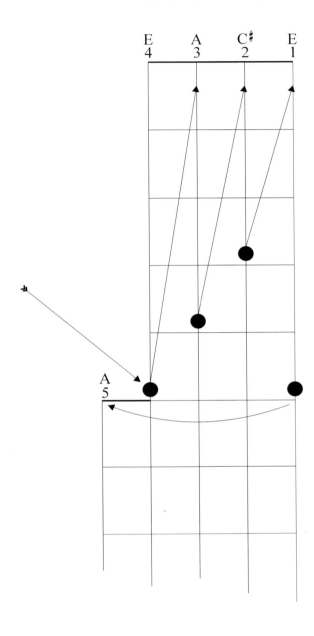

7

Chords Used in the Key of A
(Use A Tuning)

A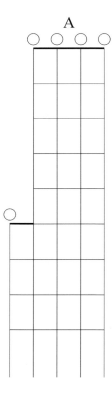

D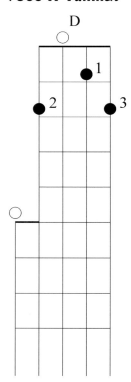

E 7th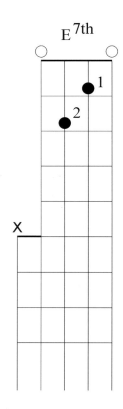

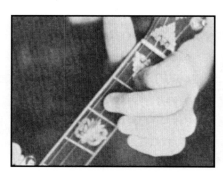

The three above chords are used mainly for old time or hill-billy songs when playing in the Key of "A". Be sure banjo is tuned for the right Key (A). The B7th chord shown at right is often played and usually followed by E7th.

When playing E7th you may omit the "thumb" string as it actually does not harmonize. However it can be picked almost at anytime if you wish.

B 7th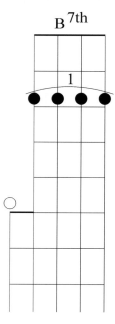

Keeping Good Time and Exercise for Picking

One of the most important things in playing music is to keep good time. Written music is divided into measures each getting the same number of counts or beats. In four-four time each measure gets four beats. In the exercise below it will help you to keep good time if you will count (mentally or aloud) 1, 2 & 3, 4 & 1, 2 & 3, 4 & etc. Keep the same speed when playing.

In this exercise we are playing the "A" chord only (A tuning).

When a note appears on the lower line it means you are to pick the 5th string with the thumb. To make it clearer the notes to be picked with the thumb are indicated with the letter "T". A note appearing on the top line means you are to strike the 1st string with your 1st finger. The 2nd line from the top represents the 2nd string, etc. When one or more notes are directly below another all the indicated strings are to be picked with one stroke of the finger. On the first count you pick the 1st, 2nd and 3rd strings open by striking across them with the finger. On the 2nd count you repeat this and also get a quick thumb note in - all on the 2nd count. The 3rd and 4th count is a repetition of the 1st and 2nd count. Count slowly until you get the idea.

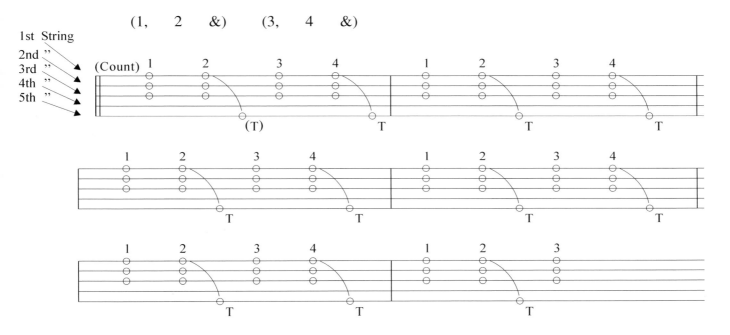

9

Bile Dem Cabbage Down

(A Tuning)

```
        A                    D
(1st)   CORN  BLADES  RUS'LIN  IN  DE  BREEZE,

        A            E7        A
        PUNKINS  ON  DE  GROUND,  SQUIRRELS  AM

              D              A        E7        A
        CHIRPIN'  IN  DE  TREES,  BILE  DEM  CABBAGE  DOWN.

          A              D       A                    E7
(Chorus)  BILE  DEM  CABBAGE  DOWN,  BAKE  DAT  HOE  CAKE  BROWN,

        A              D
        ALL  THE  SONG  THAT  I  CAN  SING

           A       E7        A
        IS  BILE  DEM  CABBAGE  DOWN.

        A              D        A
(2nd)   BOB  WHITE  IN  DE  MEADOW,  BUCK  WHEAT

              E7        A              D
        TURNIN'  BROWN,  BRUDDER  POSSUM  FAT

                A       E7        A
        AND  FINE,  BILE  DEM  CABBAGE  DOWN.

        A              D       A
(3rd)   SPARE  RIBS  IN  DE  OBIN,  'TATERS  ALL

        E7        A                    D
        AROUND,  BUTTERMILK  AND.  CORN-BREAD  TOO,

        A          E7        A
        BILE  DEM  CABBAGE  DOWN.
```

How to Tune the Banjo by Ear
(D Tuning)

The D tuning is the same as the "A" tuning excepting the 4th string which is tuned 2 frets lower (The 4th string is lowered from "E" to "D".)

Or you can tune as follows: Tune the 4th string low as possible but not so low that it will rattle or not sound clear. Then place finger on 7th fret as shown here in the diagram. Then tune open 3rd string to sound the same. Next place finger on 4th fret of the 3rd string - tuning open 2nd to the same pitch. Next place finger on 3rd fret of 2nd string - tuning open 1st to sound same. Lastly - place finger on 5th fret of 1st string - tuning open 5th string to sound the same.

You can also tune to a piano as shown below.

For playing in the key of D

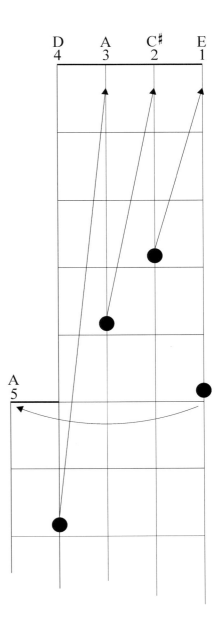

11

Chords Used in the Key of D

D

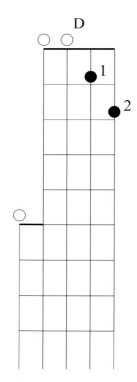

G

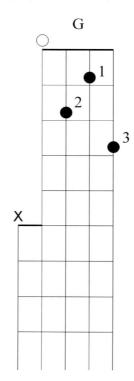

A ^{7th}

A ^{7th}

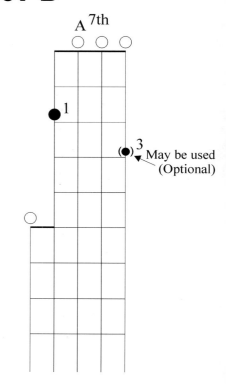

(●)³ ← May be used (Optional)

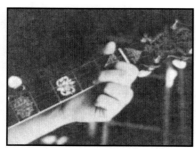

E ^{7th}

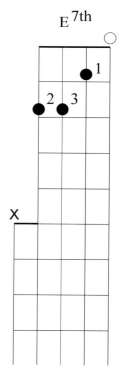

The "E7th" chord is sometimes used when playing in the key of "D" and is usually followed by "A7th".

Ring De Banjo
(D Tuning)

By Stephen Foster

           D

(1st)   DE TIME IS NEBBER DREARY IF DE DARKEY

             A7   **D**

NEBBER GROANS;   DE LADIES NEBBER WEARY

                  A7   **D**

WID DE RATTLE OB DE BONES.   DEN COME

                                      A7

AGAIN SUSANNA, BY DE GASLIGHT OB DE MOON;

          D

WE'LL TUM DE OLD PIANO

                A7   **D**

WHEN DE BANJO'S OUT OB TUNE

        D

(Chorus) RING, RING DE BANJO!   I LIKE DAT

               A7

GOOD OLD SONG.

        D

COME AGAIN MY OWN TRUE LUB!

               A7   **D**

OH, WHA YOU BEEN SO LONG ?

How to Tune the Banjo by Ear
(G or C Tuning)

This is the same as "A" tuning except that the 5th string is tuned 2 frets lower from A to G.

Or you can tune as follows: -
Tune the 4th string low as possible but not so low that it will rattle or not sound clear. Then place finger on 5th fret and tune open 3rd to sound the same. Next - place finger on 4th fret of 3rd string tuning open 2nd to the same pitch. Next - place finger on 3rd fret of 2nd string tuning open 1st to the same pitch. Lastly - place finger on 3rd fret of 1st string and tune 5th string to sound the same.

You can also tune to the piano as shown below.

1st string   2nd   3rd   4th   5th

For playing in the keys of G or C

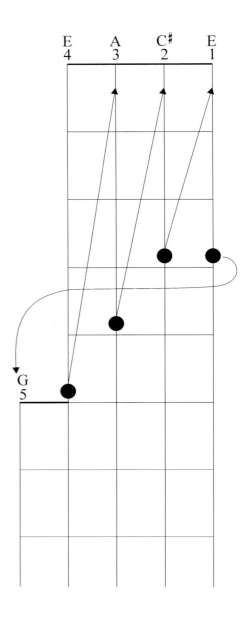

Chords Used in the Key of G
(Use G Tuning)

G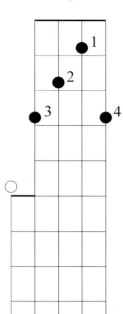

C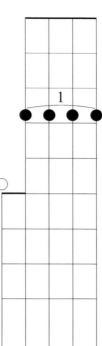

D⁷ᵗʰ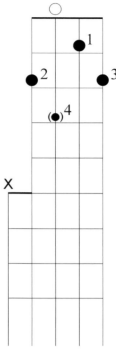

The "A7th" chord is sometimes used when playing in the key of "G" and is usually followed by "D7th".

A⁷ᵗʰ

15

Golden Slippers
(G and C Tuning)

```
                      G
(Verse)   OH  MY  GOLDEN  SLIPPERS  AM  A-LAYED  AWAY


                                                D7
          'CAUSE  I  DON'T  'SPECT  TO  WEAR  'EM  TILL  MY  WEDDIN'  DAY
          AND  MY  LONG  TAILED  COAT  THAT  I  LOVE  SO  WELL


                                              G
          I  WILL  WEAR  IN  THE  CHARIOT  IN  THE  MORN.
          AND  MY  LONG  WHITE  ROBE  THAT  I  BOUGHT  LAST  JUNE


                                        D7
          I'M  GWINE  TO  GET  CHANGED  'CAUSE  IT  FITS  TOO  SOON
          AND  THE  OLD  GREY  HOSS  THAT  I  USED  TO  DRIVE


                                                    G
          I  WILL  HITCH  HIM  TO  THE  CHARIOT  IN  THE  MORNING.



          G                                  C
(Chorus)  OH,  DEM  GOLDEN  SLIPPERS,  OH,  DEM  GOLDEN  SLIPPERS,


          D7
          GOLDEN  SLIPPERS  I'SE  GWINE  TO  WEAR


            G
          BECAUSE  THEY  LOOK  SO  NEAT.


                                    C
          OH,  DEM  GOLDEN  SLIPPERS,  OH  DEM  GOLDEN  SLIPPERS,


          D7
          GOLDEN  SLIPPERS  I'SE  GWINE  TO  WEAR


                                G
          TO  WALK  THE  GOLDEN  STREETS.
```

Chords Used in the Key of C
(Use C Tuning)

C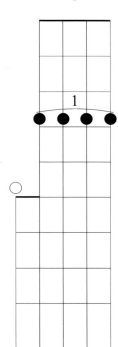

F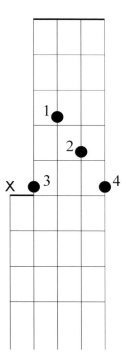

G⁷ᵗʰ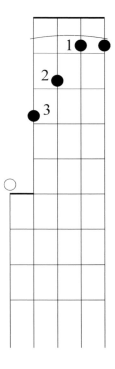

The "D7th" chord is sometimes used when playing in the key of "C" and is usually followed by "G7th".

D⁷ᵗʰ

17

Oh! Susanna
(G and C Tuning)

By Stephen Foster

```
            C                                                    G7
(1st)   I  COME  FROM  ALABAMA  WITH  MY  BANJO  ON  MY  KNEE;

            C                                         G7         C
        I'SE  GWAN  TO  LOUSIANNA  -  MY  TRUE  LUB  FOR  TO  SEE,
        IT RAINED ALL NIGHT DE DAY I LEFT, DE' WEDDER

            G7          C
        IT  WAS  DRY;  THE  SUN  SO  HOT  I  FROZE

                        G7          C
        TO  DEF,  SUSANNA,  DON'T  YOU  CRY.

        F                    C              G7
(Chorus) OH !  SUSANNA,  DON'T  YOU  CRY  FOR  ME

            C                                      G7        C
        I  COME  FROM  ALABAMA,  WID  MY  BANJO  ON  MY  KNEE,

            C
(2nd)   I  HAD  A  DREAM  DE  UDDER  NIGHT  WHEN  EBRY -

            G7          C
        TING  WAS  STILL;  I  THOUGHT  I  SAW  SUSANNA

                        G7          C
        DEAR  A-COMING  DOWN  THE  HILL. THE  BUCK
        WHEAT  CAKE  WAS  IN  HER  MOUF,  DE  TEAR  WAS

            G7          C
        IN  HER  EYE.  SAYS I,  I'SE  COMING  FROM  DE

                        G7          C
        SOUF,  SUSANNA  DON'T  YOU  CRY.    (Repeat Chorus)
```

MRS. GRANDPA (RAMONA) WITH HER FIDDLE

A COUPLE OF OLD TIMERS

Transposing Chart

Showing which chords to play when changing to another key.

	1	2	3	4
Key of "A" ——	A	D	E^{7th}	B^{7th}
Key of "D" ——	D	G	A^{7th}	E^{7th}
Key of "G" ——	G	C	D^{7th}	A^{7th}
Key of "C" ——	C	F	G^{7th}	D^{7th}

Examples:

To change chords of song from key of "A" to key of "D" ----

Where A chord is shown use chord in column 1 across from key of "D" which is D chord. Likewise instead of D play G, etc.

To change chords of song from key of "G" to key of "A" ----

Instead of G chord in column 1 play A in column 1. In place of D7 play E7 in column 3, etc.

You can soon learn by memory or by "ear" which chords to use.

When singing or humming a song you will learn to select a key which puts your voice in the right range. That is to play in a key so that you can reach the highest and lowest notes in the song without placing too much strain on your voice. Play a chord or two of each song in a different key until you find the key best suited to your voice.

As shown below (o) on a string means to play it open.

(•1) means to press finger on 1st fret
(•2) means to press finger on 2nd fret, etc.

Press firmly just behind fret indicated so that you can get a clear tone.

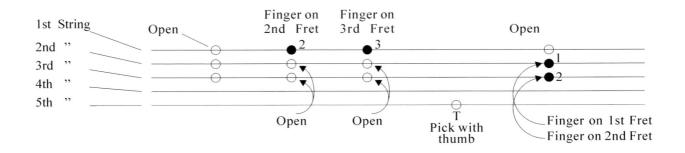

Old Joe Clark
(Solo) A Tuning

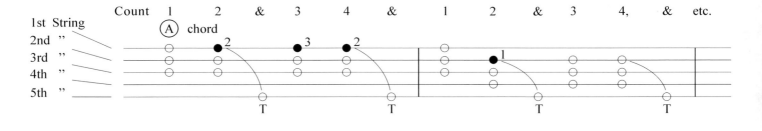

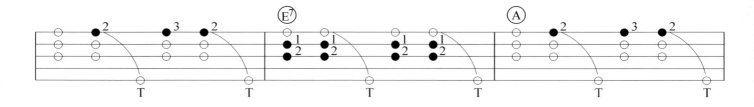

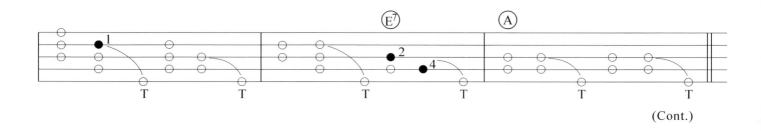

(Cont.)

Old Joe Clark (Continued)

(Chorus)

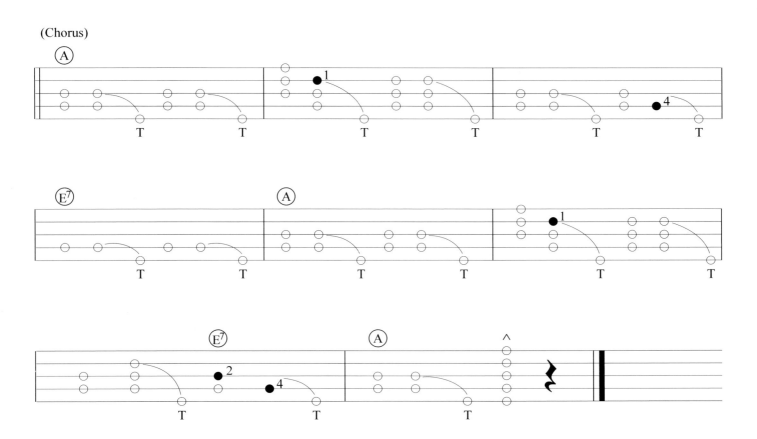

The above arrangement makes use of full harmony. You might try playing just the top note of each chord. At the same time alternate the thumb note on another string. That is: first time pick the thumb note on the 5th string. Second time pick the thumb note on 4th string. Next time back to 5th string, etc.

Using the instructions in this book as a guide to get started and learn the fundamentals of playing the banjo you will develop your own style with practice and experience.

Pretty Little Pink

(A Tuning)

              A
(Chorus) OH FLY AROUND MY PRETTY LITTLE MISS

FLY AROUND MY DAISY

FLY AROUND MY PRETTY LITTLE MISS

       E7   **A**
YOU ALMOST DRIVE ME CRAZY !

             A
(Verse) HER CHEEK AS RED AS A RED, RED ROSE

HER EYES AS A DIAMOND BROWN

GOIN' TO SEE MY PRETTY LITTLE MISS

   E7   **A**
BEFORE THE SUN GOES DOWN,

A
(Verse) COFFEE GROWS ON WHITE OAK TREES

THE RIVER FLOWS WITH BRANDY

ROCK ON THE HILLS ALL COVERED WITH GOLD

       E7   **A**
AND THE GIRLS ALL SWEETER THAN CANDY.

GRANDPA BEFORE AND AFTER 1930

Darby's Ram
(D Tuning)

            D
(1st)   OLD   DARBY   LIVED   ACROSS   THE   CREEK

                                       A7
AND   WHEN   HE   TOLD   A   TALE

D
EV'RY   MINNOW   IN   THAT   CREEK

                            A7   **D**
GOT   BIGGER   THAN   JONAH'S   WHALE.

            D
(Chorus) OH,   WASN'T   HE   A   BIG   UN,   BOYS,

            D   **A7**
OH,   WASN'T   HE   A   BIG   UN,   BOYS,

                                 G
OH,   WASN'T   HE   A   BIG   UN,   BOYS,

   D   **A7**   **D**
BEFORE   THEY   CUT   HIM   DOWN.

            D
(2nd)   MY   GRAND   DAD   HAD   AN   OLD   BUCK   SHEEP,

                                 A7
I   STILL   CAN   HEAR   HIM   SAY

D
ONE   OF   THE   FINEST   RAMS,   SIR,

                       A7   **D**
THAT   EVER   WAS   FED   ON   HAY.

Photo by Les Leverett

Camptown Races
(D Tuning)

          D
(Verse) DE CAMPTOWN LADIES SING THIS SONG,

A7   **D**
DOO DA, DOO DA, DE CAMPTOWN RACE TRACK

                       A7   **D**
NINE MILES LONG -- O DOO DA DAY.

        D
I CAME HERE WID MY HAT CAVED IN,

A7   **D**
DOO DA, DOO DA, I GO BACK HOME WID MY

                    A7   **D**
POCKET FULL OF TIN, O DOO DA DAY.

D   **G**
(Chorus) GWINE TO RUN ALL NIGHT, GWINE TO RUN

        D
ALL DAY. I'LL BET MY MONEY ON THE

              A7   **D**
BOB-TAILED NAG, SOMEBODY BET ON DE BAY.

Photo by Les Leverett

Crawdad Song

(G and C Tuning)

(1st)

G
YOU GET A LINE - I'LL GET A POLE, HONEY

                                                               D7
YOU GET A LINE - I'LL GET A POLE, BABE

G   C
YOU GET A LINE - I'LL GET A POLE, WE'LL GO

                                G   D7   G
DOWN TO THAT CRAWDAD HOLE, HONEY BABY MINE,

(2nd)

G
SEE THAT MAN WITH A SACK ON HIS BACK, HONEY

                                             D7
SEE THAT MAN WITH A SACK ON HIS BACK, BABE

G
SEE THAT MAN WITH A SACK ON HIS BACK, HE'S

   C
GOT MORE CRAWDADS THAN HE CAN PACK,

G   D7   G
HONEY BABY MINE.

(3rd)

G
SELL MY CRAWDADS TWO FOR A DIME, HONEY

                                        D7
SELL MY CRAWDADS TWO FOR A DIME, BABE

G
SELL MY CRAWDADS TWO FOR A DIME, YOUR

C
CRAWDADS AIN'T AS GOOD AS MINE,

G   D7   G
HONEY BABY MINE.

Photo by Les Leverett

31

Mark Jones

Mark A. Jones, son of the legendary Grandpa Jones, grew up in the heart of country music, Nashville, Tennessee. There he learned to play clawhammer style banjo from some of the finest. They included not only his father, Grandpa Jones, but other great talents such as: Bashful Brother Oswald, Stringbean, and Merle Travis. Mark began teaching banjo in 1978, passing along the traditional style to others and continues to do so today. He currently resides in the foothills of the beautiful Ozark Mountains, Mountain View, Arkansas